Destiny Man

Qualities to Look For

Kathy Gibson

Dedication

I thank my God for inspiring me to write, and who has given me all things to enjoy in Christ Jesus. Lord you are the BEST. You make all things possible and I give you all the glory.

My mother Apostle Helen Saddler, who has always believed in me. I am grateful for your encouragement, your leadership and inspiration. Along with my Heavenly Father you are the reason I kept the faith and believe I can do whatever I put my mind to do. You taught me to soar and take the limits off. I love you mom, thank you.

To my family and friends, thank you for your support and encouraging words. To Into His Chamber Global International Ministries, y'all are a blessing. Thank you.

Table of Contents

Acknowledgment

Thank you Into His Chamber's Photography Team

Michael Benjamin

Donna Anderson

Chalicia Fields

Foreword

This book is riveting and definitely thought provoking concerning the right individual that you would desire in your life. Destiny Man Qualities to Look For, is a very strategic guide that makes you internalize your search. What we are is what we look for. What we have been through becomes our comfortable and familiar zone. Pastor Kathy teaches us to understand who we are so that we will know the magnitude of who we draw into our lives and why!

Destiny Man Qualities to Look For will challenge your desires for a true mate and cause you to examine triggers from previous failed relationships. This close examination will bring awareness and solutions into knowing and growing who you are and whom you have become. Therefore, who enters your life has to be equipped to handle the weight of your value. Once you learn your value, your standard will stand absolutely strong. This straight forward book is a manual that will assist you in looking for your destiny man, because now you know what to look for!

Apostle Helen Saddler
Into His Chambers Global Int'l Min
Federal Way, Washington

III

Introduction

Ladies there is a Kingdom Man, original and designed just for you. The one that only your rib will fit as Eve's rib fit only Adams. This is the reason I was inspired to write this book.

I have seen and was once a woman who did not understand or know her value. A woman who doesn't understand her worth is vulnerable, susceptible to toxic, abusive, down-grading and dangerous relationships.

In order to discover your true identity and authenticity, you have to seek Jesus. God knows your original makeup, the person, the woman. You are a diamond in the rough, a royal diadem, you are woman extraordinaire! Because He's the master creator, you are a masterpiece, created in His likeness and image.

Women, we are from all walks of life, we have different backgrounds, different testimonies, and survived different trials. No testimony can be belittled because it has its own impact. We all have a story that can lift and encouragement someone going through.

The woman scorned is now a woman who knows her worth, her value and knows she's necessary. She's a woman whose head was once held low, battered, and bruised. And now she holds her head high because she understands the ultimate price Jesus paid for her. No one can take away her validation.

She has met her Lord and Savior. She's healed and whole, because of His love for her and her love for Him. They have a relationship. Intimacy is built, through the Word and prayer with her Lord. He is her infinite God, so she's always discovering the love, beauty, and power that she possesses. She is true royalty, a kingdom heir.

In order to know what to look for in a man, you have to know yourself, your makeup. What makes you click on or click off? How you discover yourself is by paying attention to yourself. What are your likes and dislikes? What is your personality, your temperament? What is your belief system and values? Do you love yourself, embrace your uniqueness?

Hobbies for instance, what do you enjoy? Is it shopping, reading, traveling, dancing, going to plays, to the opera? Are you a daring person, risk taker, or do you play it safe? Are you an introvert or an extrovert? Do you love yourself enough to celebrate you?

I think I can be both, some who know me may beg to differ (smile). I like to be low key at times, and other times I love to have a great time enjoying life. You have to know yourself to choose the right and healthy companionship, friendships, business partners and social groups.

I love happy endings, endings where at the end, everything comes together. Everything looked impossible at first, then, BAM, success! And give me comedy any day. I love to laugh and be around humorous but balanced people! Those who are positive, witty, and versatile; not limited. Girlfriends who you can do spontaneous things with like go on cruises, rent a limousine and have a girl's night out, or dress in elegant gowns and go to an opera. Go horseback riding or travel. Spa days are always relaxing and a great way to pour into ourselves.

I'm laughed at a lot about wanting to go skiing and bungee jumping. And I will. See you have to have the right class of like-minded influence around you. Ladies you have to get out and see, discover, explore, and learn new things, people, and places! Find out your weaknesses and strengths and let your strength outweigh your weakness.

See how you get along with other women. How are you with people in general? With other ladies are you confident in yourself to compliment them or are you insecure only see the worst in them? Do you compete or complete?

Do you always have to out-do, doing the extreme, trying to be accepted because all along you have to prove yourself? You have to be honest with yourself and confront the real issues about you. Are you a controller, superficial and bullying because deep down you struggle with fear and insecurities? What about bitterness, are you a bitter woman filled with unforgiveness?

Ladies when was the last time you touched the hem of Jesus' garment and was made whole? The healed woman is a powerful woman. She has learned to trust her Savior, her Redeemer by receiving His unconditional love and let Him into her heart.

May reading this book inspire you to search within yourself, your desires, values, and what's important to you in finding the Destiny Man that God has for you. You may see where you want to spend more quality time in discovering yourself, your uniqueness, and know your personal makeup. The powerful woman that you are. May you discover your worth and decide settling for just anything or anyone is not an option. The price in waiting on God to send you your Destiny Man is far too costly to just settle.

Like the Song of Solomon, it's not a book of many chapters like the book of Psalms. It is still and always will be the best intimate love story in history. It's one of the most romantic love stories a person can read. Filled with love and passion. The bridegroom and the bride and how he lavished her with his love and desires for her. That's how God loves his church. My prayer is that you will be just as blessed as I was in God sharing His desires for us to have His best.

1

A Man After God's Heart

"I have found David the son of Jesse, A man after my own heart." 1 Samuel 13:14.

Ladies, there's nothing like a man whose heart is after and like God's. He's a worshiper. He knows how to get into the heart of God and join with the heart of God. He's loving, caring, compassionate, and tender. He's the perfect gentleman. His love is unconditional.

A heart after God is birthed out of fellowship and relationship with Him. When you begin to experience the mercy God bestows upon you, and you know you've messed up, did some damage — those secrets you know only He knows, but He's still merciful and forgiving and has a love so deep and powerful because that's who He is. There's no hate in God because He is love. Wow, meditate on that. Lord, I thank you!

The man after the heart of God and with the heart of God is a man who has captured God's heart and God captured his heart. This man has a servant's heart. He's a man who serves. Not only does he serve, but he understands love.

King David not only was mantled with the king's anointing, but he was also mantled as a worshiper who knew how to move the heart of God. Who else would know how to get to a woman's heart than a man who knows how to worship his Lord. A sensitive and masculine man who breaks before the Lord. Ladies the yielded man is a man strong in the Lord and yet a humbled man.

As a man of prayer, a worshiper, a throne room man, that's a man after the heart of God. He's a covenant man. He knows God to be a covenant God, a man who's not afraid of commitment. Um! Ladies, I told you they do exist. The Holies of Holies man. Oh my God!

Do you know what kind of Destiny Man this is? He's one who is taught by the Master himself, how to love. "Husbands love your wife as Christ loves the church...." Ephesians 5:25, so in prayer, he's taught how to be a loving husband, a selfless man, learning how to give from the Giver himself. He knows how to be a provider, a husband, a father. He's a responsible man.

Because of his relationship, intimacy with the Lord, he wears the Lord's mantel, he is a God-fearing man.

2

The Man at The Gate: Can He Cover You?

"Her husband is known in the gates when he sitteth among the elders of the land." Psalm 31:23.

The gate represents the kingdom, government, the home. When you have gated homes, only certain people have access to enter. The man watches and covers the gate and has authority on who can and cannot enter. The gate represents covering and protection. Do you know what's about to cover you?

The oil on his head (what oil has God poured on his head?) He is a man who can protect his family. He watches over his family, he watches what comes in and what goes out. He is the watchman of his gate. He's able to stand at the gate.

Protector from the enemy, he's a Seer in the spirit. Seers in the Bible represent prophets. He's a man who can see in the realm of the spirit and decree and declare. Any time he leaves his post at the gate as your leader, your king, your headship, he leaves everyone he's to protect open for attacks. When the head is off balance then so is

9

everyone that comes under the umbrella of his covering. Ladies, know what legacy (his lineage) is going to cover you.

As a provider, husband, father, prayer partner and your best friend, there are responsibilities that are for the man to handle. He is fashioned that way. No matter how much a woman is forced or not forced into the position to carry the load of the head, the man has his place.

The man at the gate understands and knows how to get access through the gate and how to get the gate open. See ladies you have to have a man that sits at the gate and has access to get in the gate. You have to be some kind of woman, some kind of diamond; you have to know your womanhood, your worth, your value.

You have to know your favor for him to obtain it from the Lord. Like Hannah, you have to be a woman at the gate of intercession. Like Ruth and Esther, they went through the process of purification to birth this type of anointing. When Ruth's husband died, she didn't leave Moab right away. When she went to Bethlehem, she went through detoxification. Before she went to Boaz, Naomi told Ruth to anoint herself. Ruth prepared herself for her covering.

Esther went through a year of purification for King Xerxes. She went through a crushing before coming to the palace. Crushing is like the olives that produce oil. Royalty takes a special kind of anointing to handle. She was raised by her uncle Mordecai. Then she went through another crushing with frankincense and myrrh. That crushing produced an anointing and fragrance that lingered in the atmosphere wherever she went. Not only that, but she had a fragrance that captured the King's heart.

3

The Mentored Man

Give instruction to a wise man, and he will be yet wiser:
teach a just man, and he will increase in learning.
Proverbs 9:9

The mentored man is a confident man, a processed man, trained by a seasoned mentor. Ladies to have a seasoned mentored man is priceless, he carries a different oil due to the crushing process.

These are your pedigree. He's trained differently, he's sat under leadership, he's been taught how to lead, to handle responsibility. He's a man with solid foundations. He understands his manhood. Destiny Men who are mentored are not common they're your uncommon men.

Mentored men understand their makeup as a man, his strengths and his weakness', which makes him a confident man. He knows what he wants. He knows how to make decisions.

He understands his role as a man, a provider and pre-visionary. He's been taught to be a man of integrity and character, a man of principle and standard. He's a responsible man. There is nothing worse than a person who is irresponsible. The mentored man is a decision maker. He's powerful. He's a man that has been groomed to be a man. He knows how to handle life situations.

There are many reasons a man if not properly guided, can be irresponsible. One reason is he hasn't been taught or hasn't had a male figure around him. Fear can be a factor as well as laziness or procrastination. In the last chapter, I asked questions to help you understand what you want. Do you know if he's a momma's boy and that's someone you would consider? Is he an only child? If he has not been taught responsibility, or how not to be selfish you will have something on your hands. A mentor in his life can lead him in the right direction.

He's taught how to be a gentleman, how to be a refined man. Kingdom pedigrees are bred differently. They are taught discipline; they have etiquette skills. Ladies, you need to know what to look for. These are rare breeds.

Just like the Proverbs 31 woman, Ruth, Esther and Mary who were overshadowed by the Lord. These men do exist. Like the Proverbs 31 woman, who is rare.

"Who can find a virtuous woman for her price is far above rubies." I feel the mantel – that crown resting already. He's a man of virtue. He's a man who's been through the process.

4

Man of Vision

"Write the vision, and make it plain upon tablets, that he may run that readeth it." Habakkuk 2:2,3.

He's a visionary, for his empire and his family. He can stand alone but understands it not good for man to be alone. To attract a kingdom - dominion man, a man of vision, you need a man who knows and see where he's going and understands his purpose. He is a purpose-driven man. Ladies to attract the kingdom vision man, you have to be a kingdom vision woman. What is your God-inspired vision? Once you know your purpose and vision, you will attract your Destiny Man.

You have to know where and what you want in life. Without knowing, your road in life can be fatal. You will always attract wrong relationships, not just with the opposite sex but in general. Always wrong choices, in jobs, geographically, and the list can go on, unless or until you know your true purpose. Vision begins with you. Write the vision and start your journey to success and attract kingdom destiny relationships.

He's a visionary man with a plan. He's a planner and he's focused. Do you know where he wants to be in five years, ten years? What is his vision for a family, career, is he planning to own a home or real estate. Not only does he have a family plan, does he have a business plan? Are you looking to have your own business? What are his goals? And will your vision and the vision he has be something that will work for the both of you? Or you may join together? Visionaries are strong leaders, they prioritize, they're relentless, they are builders. Visionaries attract visionaries.

5

The Warrior Man of Prayer

*"Now when Solomon had made an end of praying, the
fire came down from heaven, and consumed the burnt
offering and the sacrifices; and the glory of the LORD
filled the house." 2 Chronicles 7:1*

Ladies, a man of prayer is a fragrant man. Yes,
Lord! Ladies the man in the presence of God, whew let's
have some fun yet serious. Ladies not only does he wear
the finest colognes and dress in the finest of fashion. This
fragrant man is the man of integrity of character, filled
with the spirit of God.

A man of prayer is not an empty man of voids and
holes in his soul. A man with a prosperous soul is
powerful and anointed. This is why the wait is worth it.
And you are worth the wait!

He is a king. He's royalty. Who dwells in the
presence of the King of King. He's a king that the
presence of the King rests on. Because of his relationship
with the King, he has the kingship anointing. When he
speaks, there is power and authority. Ladies, why would

you want anything less than a man whose heart is after the King of Kings and the Lord of Lords?

And a man who knows how to war and win in prayer? Who knows how to shift atmospheres, dethrone demonic principalities, wicked spirits in high places, he walks in power and authority. When he comes out from being in the throne room, God is all on him. His voice releases a sound that commands attention, and when he speaks, it's the sound of the Lion of Judah.

He is a warrior in the realm of the spirit and realm of prayer, A man with battle scars where he has conquered and defeated the enemy. Give me a God-Man who knows how to war in the spirit. Who knows how to get a breakthrough. I'm talking about the faith man, which you'll read in chapter seven. He's a man who is keen in the realm of the spirit, because of his intimate relationship with Lord.

The throne room man is one drenched with oil, new wine, he's one who out of being in the presence of the Lord, is filled with downloads from glory, a man of spiritual and natural substance. He's creative.

The God encountered man is a carrier of the Shekinah and Kabode Glory of God! Where the weight of the Lord rests. Meaning he has some weight about him, some God substance. A man of wisdom, revelation, and knowledge a worshiper. He has the ear of the learned; He knows how to hear the voice of the God.

It's what you birth out of His presence. You think it's something for the woman who has captured the heart of God and had the Spirit of God. Get that man of God that has captured and caused God to turn, pause and impart.

Download into him from being in His presence. I think there's a realm we can enter and when we come out, it releases an ark anointing. Ladies, birth that king, God said ALL things are possible. Take the limits off.

6

Man of The Word

"Husbands, love your wives like Christ loved the church and gave himself up for her, so he might sanctify her, cleanse her, purify her by washing her with the water of the Word." And "Also, husbands should love their wives like their bodies." Ephesians 5;26.

Ladies if he doesn't love himself then he won't have the ability to love you. A man who loves his wife is a man who loves himself. Because he is a man who values himself, his temple, he will honor and respect your temple. He won't ask for what he won't commit to in marriage. You're worth it!

He is a man of the Word, one who reads, meditates, and follows scripture. A man of the Word is a man of faith and can hear. He understands his role as a spiritual headship of his home, first with himself, wife and children and career.

Because he knows the Word, he can sustain his wife and family. He knows the Word works in every area of his life and means wellbeing for both him and his family. He is a hearer and a doer of God's Word. He knows the Word is a weapon to the enemy and blessing to Him. To know the Word is to sanctify your wife, you can go deep. The power of him being a man of the Word, it's like holy hyssop, it torments the devil. He understands who the Word is.

He has the wisdom, understanding, knowledge, revelation, and language of the kingdom, because of prayer and the Word.

7

Man of Faith

"Without faith, it's impossible to please God."
Hebrew 11:16.

He is a man who believes what is impossible for man is possible with God. He believes in the realm of faith due to his relationship in prayer, knowing through his relationship with God, he's experienced the faithfulness of God. He's communed with God to know God will never leave him nor forsake him, according to Hebrews 13:5. He relies upon and trusts in God for all his decisions. He's seen Him countless times move on his behalf.

He knows the power that faith manifests. He has faith in the realm of all things are possible. A man of faith is a man who can stand when adversity arises; he's stable in his ways.

Visionary men are men of strong faith, which makes them relentless in their endeavors. He understands the power he has to call those things that be not in existence because of his realm of faith. He understands that the power of faith moves obstacles. A man of faith is a conqueror. He faces the giants. He's a man of tenacity.

He doesn't give up. A man of faith goes in strong pursuit of his dreams and passion. He's not wavering or double minded in his faith with God. He is relentless. He's unstoppable, he's not moved by the storms that come, he's like an eagle that rises above the storm. He understands his faith is strengthened with the storms. When all odds are against him, he still stands on what he believes. His faith is fearless like the lion. To reach his destiny he knows it takes faith.

8

The Man Anointed for You

*"Thou anointest my head with oil; my
cup runneth over." Psalms 23:5*

Ladies even though it's said, you are made for
each other, or compatible, I believe when God sends and
gives you your Destiny Man, being anointed for one
another takes the relationship deeper. Even though both
of you have gone through processes to get here. There's
another process it will take in holy matrimony when you
come together as one.

The power of God's anointing and being carriers
of His anointing, will destroy yokes and barriers. By this
time generational curses on both sides have been dealt
with during the processing time, negative attitudes,
drama, idiosyncrasies, pride, etc.

That's why the purification process is very
necessary. When marriage comes, you are able to handle
the enemy that comes against marriages. See this is
different from the one that attacks singles. He knows the

power of when two come together; he knows the power of agreement. A house divided cannot stand.

That's why you are anointed with each other and with both anointing's joined, you are a terror to the enemy; weapons of mass destruction. Together you are a force to be reckoned with. Dominating forces that are unstoppable. That's why you have to know your position and worth in Christ. We are called the bride of Christ. God takes marriage seriously.

That man is anointed for you. Anointed to handle your vulnerability and strength, anointed to protect and shield. He's anointed to intercede, anointed to speak a word and prophecy. Ladies, he's anointed to love you. Catch it, ladies, the Song of Solomon. Anointed to make you laugh and cry, no one can get to you like someone you love. The Destiny Man is anointed for you!

9

The Man, The Leader

"For the husband is the head of the wife, even as Christ is the head of the church: and he is the saviour of the body." Ephesians 5:23

A Man who cannot lead or provide for his own, especially for those of his own house, is a man who lacks the faith.

Ladies, you want a man who is a leader, a decision maker, when he speaks his voice carries weight, you trust his leadership. What are his values? Go back to the man with a vision, he can't lead if he's unable to see where he's going or know where he's going. Is he able to provide for himself? How does he manage his finances? Can he afford you and a family? Is he a stable man? Is he a man of principles?

Ladies is he able to provide? Ladies let's start right here. If he can't provide for himself, he's struggling mentally, spiritually, physically, lacking prosperously in his soul realm. Then somewhere he lacks faith. He's unequipped to handle the responsibilities it takes to provide for you or a family.

I've seen a woman who doesn't know their worth get men without jobs, living on their mama. The boyfriend is driving their vehicle. He is staying at home while she goes to work, playing video games, eating up everything. Oh no! You've seen it. How can he lead you and he hasn't gotten himself together? Destiny Men are leaders who lead, that's what they do; it's in their DNA.

Don't get me wrong, we have many testimonies of people who have survived and succeeded marriages in a struggle. But they will also tell you if they had the wisdom of what they know now they would have done it differently. Wisdom can eliminate a lot of pain. Ask for wisdom.

10

The Opulent Man

"But thou shalt remember the LORD thy God: for it is he that giveth thee power to get wealth..."
Deuteronomy 8:18

An opulent man is an abundant life man. He's a man of wealth and substance, spiritually, mentally, physically and financially. Abundancy depends on what your desires are. God says, trust in Him and He'll give you the desires of your heart. As my mother says, "Don't be afraid to reach past the stars into the realm of "all things are possible."

He's your well-defined gentleman, well mannered. He's a man of stature and excellence. The opulent man is in a class by himself. He knows how to carry himself. He knows how to treat a lady, it's his character. When it's his character, he does it across the board. He treats and respects others. That's why you see how he treats his mother and father, those in authority and those less fortunate. Who are his friends? What type of company does he attract?

That's why you go through the process, discover who you are, you're worth your value; that you're fearfully and wonderfully created. And don't limit your desires, because you know who your Heavenly Father is. He's your Ishi. ISHI – The Lord, My Husband.

Because of your relationship with the Lord, He shows you how you should be treated. And he shows you your value. That's why God says, you're fearfully and wonderfully, fashionably, designer made. He's a chivalry man, the gentleman knows how to treat a godly woman. You know ladies, to each his own, you decide what your taste is. Need I say any more?

11

Power of Communication

Wisdom is the principal thing; therefore get wisdom: and with all thy getting get understanding. Proverbs 4:7

Communication is Power. Understand love language. A lot of the wrong perception, hurts, damaged relationships come from lack of communication and honesty. We tend to expect people to understand us or know what we want, or how we feel or think. How to learn to communicate effectively goes back to knowing yourself as I mentioned earlier.

Communication is vital in any level of relationships, meaning husband and wife, parents and child, business partnerships, CEO and vice president, manager, and employee. Communication is powerful; it strengthens relationships.

To communicate, you have to be open to express your likes and dislikes. You have to be honest with one another, overthrowing fears and rejection. In other words, being confident in who you are and your uniqueness.

Communicate your language; women have a different language then men, and if we learn to communicate our language, relationships can grow strong. This is done by being open to hear and listen. Not assume. Miscommunication happens when we assume a person likes, dislikes or think as we think, rather than learning that person. Then you have to accept we're different, and nothing is wrong with that.

If you don't tell me, you don't like coach cologne, and you like Gucci instead, I'll keep getting you coach, not knowing you dislike it. While wondering why I keep smelling Gucci. Two observations here, one, assuming you like what I like and two, not observing you never wear what I gave you. Communication is powerful. So is observation.

You have to be open to share and communicate on finances, family, experiences, and friendships when you're contemplating a lifetime relationship such as marriage. It's all too important to be on the same page and open to compromise at times without crossing boundaries, losing self-respect and dignity.

12

Ladies Birth Your King

The Destiny Man is birthed from the place of intimate prayer, intercession, fasting and travailing. Dwelling in the secret place of the Most High God and letting your steps be ordered by the Lord. Letting God lead and connect you to your king.

Ladies, knowing what qualities to look for happens when you know who you are. Ask yourself what kind of Destiny Man that you want and then seek God for the one He has for you. He gave Ruth a Boaz, Esther a King, and the Proverbs 31 Woman the man at the gate. As I recall, the first chapter of Proverbs was the words of a king, speaking of the prophecy his mother taught Him. It sounds like Proverbs 31 Woman had a king.

Be honest with yourself, don't just settle for anything because you are desperate or feel like you're running out of time. If this is your reason, you're not ready for the Destiny Man God has designed just for you. Let God fill those voids with Himself and allow God to heal your soul to the place of prosperity. It gives Him great pleasure for you to have a prosperous soul and health.

Now you're ready, you're on time, embrace your God-given value and uniqueness. Your magnet is strong. Know who you are, and you'll know what to attract in any relationship whether it be business, friends or your king.

Ask the tough questions. How long has it been since his last relationship? How long has he been abstinent, five, ten, twenty years? Ladies tough but needed questions to ask. Know what's about to cover you, what's in that last name. What kind of legacy is he carrying? Do a background check and family history. What's in that bloodline? That's why the process is imperative. Let God do it for you.

Study the makeup of men. Do you want a first born, middle born or last born? A balanced first born is what I like. They're leaders, visionaries, responsible because they had the responsibility of their younger siblings. They usually understand family. They've had to learn to share and give. The reason I say balanced is they have to learn to enjoy life and how to give back to themselves.

He's learned to laugh and enjoy life. Laughter is good for the soul. I love people who have a sense of humor. Ask God for what you need, remember you don't have to settle. There are all kinds of men out there, opulent or broke, distinguished, refined, well mannered, well groomed, selfless and selfish. But there's one chosen just for you.

Do you mind picking up after a man who hasn't been trained, because he never had to do for himself? Good credit, bad credit, in debt, out of debt. Do not underestimate the warning signs. Does he pay his bills on time or at all? As I mentioned before, is he stable financially and mentally? What charities does he support? Is he involved in the community?

Does he love his parents or hate his parents? How does he get along with them? Does he have father issues or mother issues? How are his people skills? How well does he get along with people? That's where you'll know where you stand with him. Do you like the doors open for you or do you push your own cart? I've gone to the grocery store and seen women push the cart and on top of that put the groceries in the vehicle while he sits in the car while she's doing it. No sir! Something to consider. Ladies the choice is up to you.

I was in love with and going to marry a man, but I was hesitant in asking critical questions because I didn't want to seem like I was after money and I didn't want to lose him, even though I was a stylist and had my own.

Ask yourself will you lose your identity and be stripped being with him. I know women who as soon as they linked up with the wrong man, it's like poverty attached to them, they went into a struggle. And he wasn't an imposter, the glory of God was on him, but he was the wrong man.

The trick of the devil was to derail them back to Egypt and from their true call and purpose. Without walking in your divine purpose, you will always have a sense of unfulfillment. Don't go back. Will he be a man who will enhance and bring out the best in you, will you prosper and flourish with him? Something to think about it.

Ladies I didn't know my worth, who I was, that I was worth those answers. Security is very important. You can't be afraid to ask if he's able to handle every day needs to live. If you can't ask and talk about financial stability, like whether he can afford a home, insurance, the maintenance it takes to have a wife and family, he isn't for you. Or if you're afraid to lose him for asking pertinent questions, he isn't for you. Do an inner security check. Build your confidence in the Lord. Your life value is too important not to ask.

You're worth it! Remember you're fearfully and wonderfully made, Jesus felt you were worth the price He paid for you. Don't be afraid to ask questions. Be confident queen.

Now Birth Your King.

About the Author

Kathy Gibson is the assistant Pastor under the leadership of Apostle Helen Saddler, founder of Into His Chambers Global International Ministries.

She is anointed and called by God. She specializes in deliverance and healing ministry. She operates in the demonstration of signs and wonders and is astutely accurate in the prophetic.

Her intimacy with the Lord has made her a prime candidate in the lives of singles for holiness and righteousness. She is an admired role model that bears gifts unto the Lord and He displays Himself openly in her ministry. Many have witnessed the fire of God, the freshness of God, the presence of God and definitely the power of God.

Pastor Kathy is sought out and in great demand. God has anointed Pastor Kathy with the mantle of wealth. She is an entrepreneur as she partners with her mother in the SHAAA, a collection of anointing oils and perfumes.

This awesome vessel had been acknowledged for her community service and rewarded for integrated programs that created jobs, assist in education and scholarship promotion. She also assists young girls into becoming poise, self-confident and God oriented ladies with her D.I.V.A. program, Divinely Inspired Virtuous and Anointed.

Contact Pastor Kathy at:
ladyopulentdestinyman1@gmail.com

Made in the USA
Middletown, DE
12 February 2020